Mexico IN MY Eyes

OWEN XU

Ordering Information:

For orders and inquiries, please contact:
1-888-375-9818
www.toplinkpublishing.com
bookorder@toplinkpublishing.com

Printed in the United States of America

To those who love or may come
to love Mexico and its culture.

Contents

About Me

I am a Chinese born in Mexico. My parents are authentic Chinese, born in China and came to Mexico in their twenties. They came here due to different reasons, however, in Mexico, they met each other, got to know each other and fell in love with each other. They went back to China to get married and then decided to come back to Mexico. Therefore, my brother and I were born here.

Now more and more Chinese coming and living here, but at that time there were not so many, and very few had their child born and grew up here. Due to the huge differences in language and eating habits, it is not easy for Chinese people to adapt to Mexican life. In addition, the educational concepts of Chinese and Mexicans are also very different, most Chinese in Mexico prefer to keep their children in China for education. My parents have hesitated after we were born, not knowing if they should let us go back to China. But my parents didn't like the idea to separate from us, so they decided to let us stay together in Mexico.

My brother and I started school at a very young age because my mom had to go to work. At that time we were the only Asian face in the school and got a lot of attention. Kids were very friendly, they came close to us to make friends. It took us only several months to be able to speak fluently in Spanish.

Now when I recall my early years in kindergarten, I am very grateful to the teachers and friends. It is your friendship and support make us quickly integrate into the life of Mexico.

María

I still remember very well María, a teacher in my first kindergarten. My brother and I were very fortunate, our unique Asian face helped us to get more attention from teachers since we knew very little Spanish, didn't know how to play with other kids, didn't understand instructions. María was one of those teachers who took me as her favorite.

I didn't remember how I was at that time, my mom always said we were really cute when we were young. María worked as a nurse in school, her job is to take care of us during lunch time, make sure we had a good meal in the dining room. After having lunch, she would play with us, tell us stories and watch us for a snap. I remember seeing her on the first day before lunch time, she happily greeted us. Of course, I couldn't understand what she said. She immediately found me at a glance, I think she must have known at first sight that I didn't speak Spanish, so she walked straight towards me and sat next to me. From that day on, every day at lunchtime, she would deliberately sit next to me, talked with me, and encouraged other kids to show me how to speak Spanish as well. I was an outgoing boy when I was little so with the help of María I quickly made friends and began to speak more and more Spanish.

During lunchtime, María went to every kid, she knelt down on her knees so that kids wouldn't have to raise high their heads to talk with her. She asked everyone if he liked today's meal. She cared about me the most because she thought it would hard for me to get used to Mexican food. Sometimes I didn't like the lunch, she would share with me her own meal brought from home, and if she noticed that I liked it, she would have me ate up all her lunch, she didn't care that she had nothing left to eat.

After having lunch, she would tell us stories. I remember one story about a boy called Kevin, who has a poor and hard-working family. Kevin's father once found a hidden door when he was working on his fields. He opened the door out of curiosity and was shocked with what he found in that door. He yelled to his family and all of them ran to him, and of course, everyone was dumbfounded. Inside the door was a big treasure with abundant gold and precious stones. Kevin's father ran into the door immediately with great excitement, and, right behind the door, there was an old man, who said to him:

-"You must take whatever you want within one minute. Otherwise, the door will be closed and you will never get out."

Of course, he didn't pay attention to it at first. The family quickly ran into the cave, grabbing gems, gold and all kind of valuable stuff as much as they could. The whole family was overwhelmed by this big luck from heaven and when Kevin's father reminded what he was told by the old man, it was too late. There were only 5 seconds left, but all of them were too far from the entrance to get out. And the old man, with a big smile on his face, rushed out just before the door closed. María brought us new stories every day, some are funny and some can make us learn, such as this one. I always wondered, how could she remember so many stories.

I regarded María as my elder sister, although she 's almost the same age as my mom. Every day when she met me at the gate of the school, she ran to me with a big smile on her face and gave me a huge hug. Thank you, María, thank you for your love.

Rodolfo

During the first three years of elementary school, I changed school every year, since my parents were always looking for a better education for me. Generally speaking, most primary school teachers are very kind and good tempered. However, there are always exceptions.

Rodolfo was my first grade English teacher. I remember the first day he came, we were just about to start the class, we were a group of 6-year-old kids, rushing into the classroom happily and full of energy, all of us jumping and yelling. Miss Andrea, the secretary of the director

Roberto, came in and told us that a new English teacher called Rodolfo arrived, "he's a great teacher with high intellectual capacities and a great sense of humor," the last part made us all happy because all we wanted was some fun. Gerard, my best friend, asked Miss Andrea kindly if we could exchange our Pokemon Cards with Mr. Rodolfo, Miss Andrea looked at him with a big smile and said: " Sure you can little Gerard"

Miss Andrea went away, leaving us screaming, jumping and laughing. Then came Mr. Rodolfo, the classroom quieted down immediately and we all smiled at him. He made a brief self-introduction, smiled a little at us, then started with the class. Ever since then, he changed to a totally different person, he lost his temper now and then, yelled at us for any tiny error we made, blaming us for being "stupid", and even threw a thick book to hit our heads. Many of us complained to our parents when we got home.

The next day, an urgent meeting was held with the director and all the parents of the class, Miss Andrea immediately took an action to fire Mr. Rodolfo.

As time went on, I gradually realized that it is a privilege to have a good teacher, with great compassion and patience, especially for those in kindergarten and Lower School. I didn't know why Mr. Rodolfo acted in such a way. Maybe it was a hard time for him, or maybe he had some personal problems that day. Anyway, he left with us with a terrible memory that cannot be erased at all.

Enrique

What does a typical history class look like? Is it a boring class in which the only thing we can do is to sit still, take notes and read the textbook quietly? Is it a class that you always want to skip? Well, let me tell you that my case is different, all because of Enrique.

Enrique was my world history teacher in 6th grade. My elder brother was in his class before and I remember my brother used to tell me how great Enrique was, and his class was the most interesting of all. I couldn't believe him, I mean, how can you imagine that World History is the best class in school? Well, when I entered 6th grade, my mindset totally changed and my love of history has been enlightened from his class.

I remember when I was reading the class schedule, I noticed that World History was arranged in the 7th class of the day, which is the penultimate class. I thought at the time that this class must be very boring just like the previous history classes I had.

When I walked into the classroom, I was immediately surrounded by a happy atmosphere, the feeling in there was just happiness. I mean, have you ever been to a place where you feel pure rejoice just for being there? Well, that was my case when I first entered Enrique's classroom. When we all sat down, we began to talk with one another. To my surprised, Enrique had a superpower to make everyone quiet without screaming or tempering like other teachers. Students had so much respect for him that when he started speaking, the students immediately shut up and quieted down. I can tell you that I never saw that in my life until then.

Enrique's passion and love of history can immediately be sensed through the way he teaches, which is indescribably amazing. He is able to mobilize everyone's interest and curiosity and make you be extremely focused on his teaching.

What I liked most about Enrique is that he compiled historical events into lifelike stories. When he told them, students could imagine themselves as if they were experiencing those historical moments. In that way, he managed to make us stay quiet, entertained, concentrated, and most importantly, he ensured that we learned and remembered.

Enrique is the best temper teacher I have ever met, or better to say, he is the most tempered teacher. He never shouts loudly, never reprimands, never punishes. when someone speaks in his class, he can always remain calm and gentle, he just says " Please keep quiet, now I am in class. Thank you." and amazingly the student will apologize and stay quiet. Sometimes, not always, he leaves homework, however, he doesn't tell you how he wants you to do it, he gives you the opportunity to do it in your own way.

Unfortunately, I only had one year with Enrique since I was changed to a new school. By the end of 6th grade, I invited him to my musical show, he accepted it with great joy. I didn't see him on the show day, but i am sure he was there and I hope he enjoyed my show.

Lunchtime!

Being a kid born in Mexico and raised in a Chinese family, I like both Chinese food and Mexican food. But my mom, most of the time, prefers to prepare Chinese food for us. So, when I was little, I used to take Chinese food as lunch to the school and I never thought it could make chaos in the school.

One day, my mom prepared a Chinese dish called Tang Yuan, which are white glutinous rice balls with sugary black sesame seeds inside, it's delicious, I really like it. My schoolmates had Mexican style lunch like Milanesa, which is thinly sliced chicken or any type of meat, fried with breadcrumbs. Fried Tacos. Quesadillas, which are corn or flour tortilla with melting cheese inside, or cheese with jam. All of them are delicious and I like them all very much.

I was the only one with a different dish, a very different dish, compared to theirs. It's like comparing cheese with milk, totally different things.

When I took my Tang Yuan to school that day, during the lunchtime, all of my classmates ran over me, they formed a crowd, surrounding me, there were kids everywhere, I didn't know what was happening, I had to take a moment to figure out what was happening. Some of them began to talk to each other, asking questions Others just watched me with huge curiosity.

I didn't understand what they were saying because at the time my Spanish was not that good. As you could imagine, they were hugely surprised when they saw my Chinese dish. Suddenly the crowd became silenced, they began to "inspect" the Tang Yuan, so many weird surprising faces appearing one after another around me. Seconds later, the crowd started to talk, again.

After the inspection of the food, they began to take a guess about what they thought the Tang Yuan could be alike. And at that moment, I was too young to understand if what they said was meant to be taken as an insult, but I took them like it. As you know, kids don't know clearly when they should take something seriously and when they should not.

Some of them said the food was owl eggs, I have no idea what an owl egg looks like, and I'm sure they haven't seen an owl egg in their life; Some of them said they were like tiny onions, which is also nonsense, onions are neither chewy, nor squishy, and most importantly, who will eat onions in water as lunch?

There came out more and more things they could find that look similar to Tang Yuan. At that time, the lunchroom was converted into a debate room for professionals. I can't help laughing every time I think about it, I can't believe they took so seriously a food as an arguing topic.

People were yelling at one another, kids were hitting each other, some were crying, because they found out that what they thought it should be, it wasn't at all. It made me cry as well, all the things they said were going after me, All the things they said, I took them very seriously, and I now know they weren't meant to be taken seriously, I was over-sensitive at that age, I took everything seriously which made really hard for me to take jokes as jokes, nothing else. After having that experience, I never took Tang Yuan as lunch again.

Today, many kids suffer from bullying, I am lucky enough that I've never experienced real bullying, but what happened to me that day, even though it's not bullying, I took it that way.

Shoelace & Stairs

Have you ever fallen accidentally because of your shoelaces? I bet you did! Falling because of your loose shoelace is practically a must be of childhood.

maybe You fell on a flatland, I wasn't that lucky. As a child, I never thought of the consequences that tiny actions could bring. I was always too lazy to tie my shoes. Mom always reminded me but I won't listen.

Once, I was finally punished by my own bad habits.

One day, in the lunchroom, I was very excited, playing happily with my friends. My shoelaces were loose but I paid no attention. I was running, going up through some stairs, and guess what? Yes! I fell... but not on a flat floor as I always did. I fell on the edge of the stair. Imagine, the stairs I fell on were basically only 3 stairs in total. But I was short, my body was only 3 stairs tall. If I were as big as I am right now, I wouldn't have even fallen on the edge of the stair, since my body is tall enough that my head wouldn't touch the stair, and I could have grab on the floor, no serious hurt for my body. But at that moment, my chin hit the stair with great force, I was running as quick as you could imagine.

I didn't understand what was happening until I felt the burn of the wound. You know when you get hurt and it feels as if your skin was getting burnt? Imagine that, my face was tiny compared to the stair, my whole chin was cut by the edge of the stair. My chin was bleeding terribly, I burst into tears and cried aloud. María and other nurses and teachers immediately called a TAXI, and my mother obviously. When the cab arrived, I was still crying, the pain was still there, and getting worse every second, but the bleeding stopped a little bit. My mother arrived, she had to carry me to the cab.

Mom was very calm, she turned to the driver and said, "To the hospital, please". She knew how grave was the wound, and when she saw it wasn't that grave, it was only a cut and some pain, she wasn't that worried. I was laid down, I looked at her face, she was serious and a little bit angry.

When we arrived at the hospital, a doctor immediately took me to his consulting room. He checked my wound for a while and told my mother it wasn't serious at all, as she expected to be. The doctor came back to me and said, "The wound needs to be sutured," obviously he was joking, but I didn't know it was a joke, I could feel an immense fear starting to grow inside me, it was getting bigger and bigger, as I was thinking of my chin getting pierced by nails, and a black string across over it. This thought was killing me, I was scared to death. But guess what, when we got out of the consulting room, he just grabbed a bottle of MOTRIN, gave me a small portion of it to drink, and a band-aid. When I saw what he gave me, I was confused, I had no idea whether he was serious or not since moments ago he told me the wound needed to be sutured.

I took the band-aid and placed it on my chin, and I swallowed my little cup of MOTRIN. Minutes later, the pain disappeared, completely.

The funny thing is that this experience made me realized the magic effect of the MOTRIN to ease pain, I took it as a great painkiller, whenever I had a headache, stomachache, the first thing I asked mom was to give me a small bottle cap of MOTRIN, I thought it could kill all kinds of pain.

Friends

Friends play an important role in the growth of a person, even if the friendship doesn't last long, you'll learn some important life lessons from it.

When I was in 3rd grade, I used to have such a friend. Let's call him A. He is as polite as most Mexican boys and looks very nice and friendly. Since I'm an outgoing person, easy to get along with, we used to get along very well, and I really took him as my best friend at that time. One day, he invited me to go to his home the next day, I was very excited and I told my mom the moment I got home. My mom was very happy as well, she signed permission so that I could leave with him the next day. But the next day when we met in school, he told me that his mom didn't allow him to invite me to his home that day, because "she preferred" another friend of his to come. I was very disappointed. Right at that time, I happened to have a severe stomachache. I was sent to the nurse room and my mom was informed to pick me up immediately. When mom arrived, I told her that I wasn't going to my friend's home, she was upset as I did and said " But his mom didn't tell me about that " I began to think it over, his mom should have informed my mom because my mom has already signed the permission to let me go with my friend and his mom, so if my mom wasn't informed about the change, nobody would come to pick me up. Then I realized that my friend lied to me. I found out later that it wasn't because his mom disagreed, but he invited another friend and didn't want me to go. I was deeply hurt and it made me realize something in real life. Sometimes, the person you love just doesn't love you back, the person you care much about just doesn't care about you at all.

When I was in lower school, I didn't care about my studies. My mom was invited to school several times by the director and psychological counselor, they all worried about my studies. My mom had a serious talk with me, but I thought they were over anxious. I told her not to worry, I'll catch up soon. Then I met my friend F, who was the best student in the class. Ever since we became good friends, my studies went better and better. I started to secretly compete with him, trying to get better grades than him, which gave me the initiative to learn. By the end of that semester, I was in the honor roll and won the first place in a spelling competition. The art of choosing a friend is crucial for one's self-development.

I consider myself as a hasty temper person. For instance, I like cooking, but I cannot wait till the food is fully cooked, I'm always eager to turn off the fire. However, quite surprisingly, I'm very patient with other people. I never thought about why I was like this before until I remember of a friend M. We used to be close friends. He suffered diabetes since he was only four years old. Due to the disease, his is easily irritated and impatient. I should be very careful not to make him angry. When he is in a good mood, he's a nice and good-grade boy. My mom always said he's so cute. Since we were good friends, I learned to take care of his emotions, and gradually I learned to be tolerant of others. Many times, even with our best friends and close families, we cannot change them to what we want them to be, we have to learn to accept what they are.

Trip to China

During the summer vacation of my second year of primary school, Mom and Dad decided to let my brother and I take a trip to China alone. The purpose of this trip was to give my brother and me an opportunity to learn how to take care of ourselves and be more independent and responsible for ourselves. We liked the idea and we were looking forward to it.

My brother was sick before the trip, so he took with him his medicine. We didn't take baggage at all since my parents thought the baggage claiming would be too much complicated for us.

On the way to the airport, I was getting nervous. Normally I was very excited when going on a family trip, but this time was totally different, we were leaving on our own! Obviously, Mom and Dad were nervous, too. There is always going to be a possibility that it does not go as you want.

We arrived at the airport, two hours earlier for our check-in, my dad did all the job literally. We slowly walked through the lonely hallways of the airport, we were seated near a small cafeteria. My dad asked us if we wanted to eat, but I didn't, as the nerves didn't let me think about anything else. All the time I was thinking of what was going to happen, how would I get to my grandparents, many questions and doubts were flowing through my head, as I walked with my family through the door of the cafeteria.

The time of flight was approaching, my heart rate was accelerating. 30 minutes to go, I said to myself, we were seated on the chairs near our departure gate. When the time's up, we followed the line and step forward slowly. Dad said to me, "Samuel, do not lose these, without them, you guys can't get back home", my heart rate raised immensely, the thought of staying in China alone was quite scaring to me.

You may be asking yourself, "What are those things your father told you not to lose?", passports, our passports. I didn't have an idea what passports mean to us at that time, but I knew I couldn't lose it otherwise I wouldn't be able to go back to Mexico.

We had our passports hanging around our neck as a necklace to avoid any accidental loss. However, I was still very worried that I would lose my passport. During the entire journey, I have been clutching my passport tightly, even not dared to close my eyes or to take a snap because I feared that it would fly away. Dad's words have been echoed in my mind all the time. When we got onto the plane, I immediately grabbed my passport and I watched my brother's one 24/7, I was very concentrated in the passports, on my mind there was only space for what my dad said, "You can't get back home without these", I was only thinking about that.

As you know, travel to China takes nearly an entire day. So when night came, my brother slept calmly in his seat, but I didn't take a bit of sleep on that flight, I grabbed my passport and my brother's. Watching them both, checking for them all the time, "Remember Samuel, without these, you can't go back home."

When we finally arrived at Beijing airport, I took both passports and kept them safely in my backpack. A lady came to us, she asked if we had our passports, perhaps because of excessive fatigue, or perhaps because of nervousness, we didn't understand her question, and we answered " No." She was terrified to hear our answer and was confused at the same time. She took us to the immigrants' office, the officers began to search for our passports, and the lady was turned to be angry when they found our passports in my backpack. Then we were allowed to leave, the lady led us out, we had no idea what was going on, what should we do, we didn't understand Chinese very much, and we couldn't ask her, that was a terrible experience.

Finally, at the end of a long elevator, we saw our aunt, waiting for us. She's like an angel, we were so happy to see her!

Children's Day

June 1st is the International Children's Day, however, Mexico doesn't celebrate it, Mexico has her own Children's Day, April 30.

Children's Day has been celebrated annually in Mexico since 1925. Children are recognized as an important part of society so the day focuses on the importance of loving, accepting and appreciating children. Schools host special events inviting parents to celebrate and share this special day with their kids. Parties are held and children take part in activities like face painting, story-telling, art workshops, and plays. A gift is a must-be for this day and children have fun all day long.

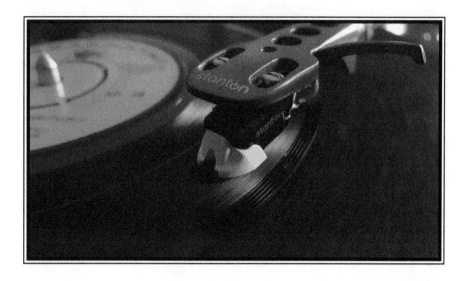

Days before Children's Day, each generation, from 1 to 6 of primary, has been assigned to a task. I remember one year, my generation was assigned to be in charge of the disco room, which was our Taekwondo room, but we converted into a disco room, where we partied for hours and hours. Another generation was in charge of the station of entertainment like the puzzle one, the haircut one, which was one of my favorites, I remember doing a haircut with my best friend Mario, a short-upwards-punk style haircut that we called the "Rhinoceros haircut".

A festival without food is not a festival, a few days before the celebration, the teacher will make a list of all kinds of foods, drinks, desserts, etc. so that everyone in the class will bring to share. If you raise your hand to bring a pizza, that's a promise for all, so you'd better keep your words and don't forget to bring it, otherwise, you'll have to eat alone, which is the saddest thing on that special day.

On Children's Day, the main focus is on the children and making them feel special. In shopping malls all over Mexico, special events with clowns, magicians, music, shows, and balloons take place. it is a festivity that is quite unique, full of laughter and play, when adults are reminded of the importance of childhood and children teach us how joyful and simple life can be. That's why when I turned to be 12, I got very sad because that was the last time for me to enjoy the Children's Day.

As per the family, China and Mexico share a very similar culture, since the family is supremely important in Mexico. There is a Grandparent's Day on August, a Family Day on the first Sunday in March, and even a day for brothers and sisters.

Day of the Dead

Mexico has tremendous cultures and traditions, one of the most well-known is the Day of the Dead. Many people think it is a Mexican version of Halloween, which is quite logical because the dates are very close. However, it isn't. Halloween is a dark night of terror and mischief, although children are all dressed up funny and cute; the Day of the Dead is a unique Mexico festival that has its profound cultural background. The Pixar movie Coco interprets the meaning very well.

Day of the Dead originated several thousand years ago with the Aztec, who considered mourning the dead disrespectful. That's why on the Day of the Dead, you don't see people crying or mourning, instead, they play music, sing, and held family parties, offer delicious food to the dead family members' tombs. They think the dead are still members of the community, kept alive in memory and spirit, so long as the memory of love still exists.

The Food of the Dead is also full of legend. According to Mexican traditional belief, the dead work up a mighty hunger and thirst traveling from the spirit world back to the realm of the living, so some families place their dead loved one's favorite meal on the altar, and the offerings must be placed one night before, leaving a whole night for the dead to "eat", and the living family must eat up all the offerings early next morning, by this way, both the living and the dead are sharing the food, as if they were together again.

The Day of the Dead is celebrated between October 31st and November 2nd. It is divided into two parts, one day is for commemorating of the dead children, another day is for commemorating of the dead adult.

In my school, we have an activity of making tombstones for one of the teachers or classmates. First, you should choose one of your favorite teachers or one of your best friends, then you need to write a "Calaverita" for him or her. Calaverita means "skull", but during the late 18th and early 19th centuries, it was used to describe short, humorous poems, which were often sarcastic tombstone epitaphs in newspapers that poked fun at the living. These literary Calaveritas eventually became a popular part of the tradition of the Day of the Dead. Once we finish our Calaverita, we need to go with our teacher and have him or her sign on it, which shows his or her consent to post it on the tombstone. Then we'll begin with our tombstone design. You can choose any material you like, for example, I used a hard paper milk box. My mom went to several cafeterias to help me to collect dozens of milk boxes. Once the body of the tombstone is done, we paste the photo of the person we have chosen and the Calaverita we wrote before. Then finally, we decorate the tombstone with flowers called Cempasuchil and a classic sugar skull.

This activity is full of fun and creativity, it took me three days to finish. The final part of this activity is voting for the best-designed and best-made tombstone, and of course, the literary Calaverita is counted as a major part of the semester grade.

Due to cultural differences and different perception of death, Chinese people are not fond of this activity. For instance, my parents used to feel very weird about it. Chinese culture believes that death is a very taboo topic. It is absolutely a big disrespect to make tombstones for living people. However, "when in Rome, do as Romans do", since we are living in Mexico, we should adapt our thinking style to Mexican culture.

Valentine's Day

Valentine's Day in Mexico is known as Dia del Amor y la Amistad, which means the day of love and friendship. It is not all about romance, like most of the other countries do, but also for friends and families. Mexicans are big fans of a holiday, so it comes as no surprise that Valentine's Day is up there as one of Mexico's favorite festivities. You'll see balloon vendors with heart-shaped balloons, fresh flowers galore for sale on streets, and chocolates selling out at shops and convenience stores. It is true that celebrating this date has no connection with Mexican history, but then again: love is a cause for celebration for all human beings and civilizations.

One traditional Mexican celebration is that teenage boys and girls, in groups divided by sex, will walk past each other in a park while heading in opposite directions. If a boy likes one of the girls, he'll hand her a flower. If the girl is still holding the flower when they pass each other later, it means she likes him back.

Well that sounds very romantic, in my school we've never had such activity, we usually have a gift exchange among classmates, we send roses to teachers, chocolates, and heart-shaped candy to loved friends, we also create hand-made cards to someone we think are special to us, and we'd love to show our affection towards them on this special day.

When I was in 5th grade, we had a very special celebration in school, which I realized later that it is not at all a newly invented celebration activity, but it was already there, and it was a very typical and unique event in the primary school in Mexico. The event is called Getting Married. A boy will invite a girl, or vice-versa, to go to a table where it says " Matrimonios " which means " Marriage " in Spanish, a teacher will sitting by that table as an official who gives authorization of marriage. The teacher will ask both of the boy and girl if they are agreed to get married, if the answer is YES, then the teacher will take out from the drawer a document and give it to the boy. This document is a contract which says " If you want to be married, you must be consent with the following requirements :

1. The husband must always receive his wife with a fully prepared delicious dinner;
2. The husband must clean dishes after dinner;
3. If you have babies, it is the responsibility for the husband to take care of them;
4. The wife is the only one who can be lazy at home.

If you agree on these terms, please sign below."

After the boy signs the document, the teacher will put a flower-adorned necklace around the neck of both and give them a ring, then the teacher will declare them as husband and wife.

That was the most fun of all the celebrations, many boys signed the contract and got married with various girls in their class. I only had one "wife" that day. when I showed my "wedding ring" and my "marriage certificate" to my parents, they couldn't help laughing.

Birthday Party

Mexican people are known for being warm, generous and above all of these, festive. They are big fans of partying. And among the parties, a birthday party is probably the most common. When I was in lower school, I was invited to a birthday party every weekend. Now you understand why Mexican children's Happiness Index is the world's No. 1. They spend most of their childhood in all kinds of birthday parties.

Mexico has several unique birthday traditions. My favorite one is "la mordida," when the birthday girl or boy's hands are tied behind their back and their face is shoved into the cake for them to take the first bite, whilst everyone around them shouts " Mordida! Mordida! Mordida!" which means "taking a bite."

Mexico is one of the few Latin countries with a birthday song that's not simply a Spanish version of " Happy Birthday." Instead, Mexico has her own birthday song called Las Mañanitas, which means the Little Mornings. A song that describes the beauty of the morning in which the singer comes to congratulate the birthday boy or girl. One of my Spanish teachers told me that the song was only sung in the morning according to an old tradition, but nowadays it can be sung at any time of the day. When the candles have been lit on the birthday cake, all the people will sing the song, and that is the most beautiful moment to remember the party.

Piñata is a must-be for a birthday party, especially for the party of small kids. The Piñata is made out of hard paper and is decorated to look like a particularly festive object or animal, or a favorite cartoon role of the birthday boy or girl. It is painted with bright colors and filled with candies and small toys. Partygoers are blindfolded and take turns to hit it trying to break open the Piñata in order to enjoy the candies and toys. My brother and I were invited to countless birthday parties, but we never liked to hit the Piñata, I guess we were the only kids who disliked it. We had odd compassion towards the Piñata, feeling sorry to watch it being hit and torn open.

Mexican Food

Many people ask me which food I like better, Chinese food or Mexican food, it's hard for me to answer, since both of them are delicious and healthy. My mom usually has Chinese food at home, when you have the same dishes all the time, you prefer to try something else, so I always buy Mexican food at school during the break.

The most well-known is the Taco, consisting of a corn or wheat tortilla folded around a filling such as beef, pork, chicken, seafood, salsa, often garnished with chili pepper, guacamole, onions. It is one of the most traditional Mexican food, and there is anthropological evidence that the indigenous people living in the lake region of the Valley of Mexico traditionally ate tacos filled with small fish. It is the favorite dish not only for me but also for my dad and my brother. My dad used to say that Taco is very similar to a typical Northern Chinese food, its flavor reminds him of his hometown. What my dad said is true, because I found out later that most of Chinese who come to Mexico like tacos just as we do, some of them even prefer to eat tacos sold on streets, they said those tacos are tastier than those sold in a restaurant.

The most popular traditional breakfast dish in Mexico is Chilaquiles. It consists of lightly fried corn tortillas cut into quarters and topped with green or red salsa. Scrambled or fried eggs and pulled chicken are usually added on top, as well as cheese and cream. It is a very healthy breakfast, I often have it as my brunch in school. Since Chinese people are generally not fond of cheese and cream, many of them don't like it very much, they think it too "strong " for their stomach as a breakfast.

Guacamole is undoubtedly one of Mexico's most popular dishes, but few people know that this traditional sauce dates back to the time of the Aztecs. It is made from mashed-up avocadoes, onions, tomatoes, lemon juice, and chili peppers. Every time I eat tacos, I'll ask for guacamole as a side dish.

Another Aztec originated food is tamales. It was a traditional food for Mayan and Inca tribes who needed nourishing food on the go to take into battle. It is made from corn dough, wrapped in banana leaves or corn husks, stuffed with either a sweet or savory filling such as meats and cheese, fruits, vegetables, chilies, and mole. It is also one of my favorite. It is quite similar to a Chinese traditional food called Zong Zi, which is made from sweet rice dough, wrapped in bamboo leaves. The filling of Zong Zi is either sweet, like a smashed red bean with sugar, or savory, like pork. So you can see, it is really hard for me to say which one I like better, I love both Chinese and Mexican food.

Sticking with food, one cultural custom many visitors find odd at first is the addition of lime and chili to EVERYTHING, and I mean it: potato chips, soups, sweets, and even fruit, no foodstuff is left behind when it comes to the addition of this condiment combo. For my brother and I, we soon get used to adding lime and chili to cucumber, mango, and corn, and we do like the taste, but for my parents, they never get used to it.

Earth Day

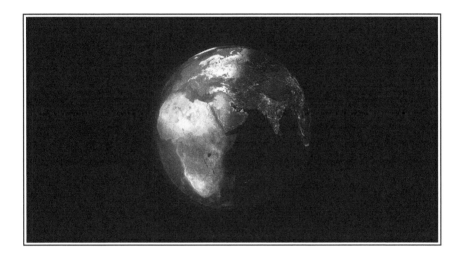

Each year, Earth Day -April 22-marks the anniversary of the birth of the modern environmental movement in 1970, which put environmental concerns on the front page.

I didn't know Earth Day until I entered middle school since there weren't any activities in lower school on this day. Generally, a science fair will be held in the school. Students participate in their own projects regarding renewable energy, green energy, etc. I was selected by my physics teacher to work together with one of my best friends for a project which will be presented in the science fair.

The project is about a bicycle with a small motor that produces electric energy with friction and movement. The motor is attached to the back wheel of the bicycle, and the bicycle is fixed on a support that makes the bicycle's back wheel to run but the bicycle will not run forward. We fixed the motor on the support, high enough that the spring part of the motor touched the wheel and turned the back wheel.

I don't know how, but my friend and I turned to be a horrible team, as we spent 90 percent of the time discussing what was the best idea, who was the correct, etc. We couldn't focus on work until the final 30 minutes, we finished the project on time as if nothing had happened.

The same thing happened before. Once we had to build a hydraulic door, a door that basically functions by water pressure. We spend literally 3 hours doing nothing but arguing with each other, then our moms called us to tell us that they were on their way to pick us up, we became super productive and finished it in 10 minutes. We could have finished it in 10 minutes, but we had it finished in 3 hours and 10 minutes.

We finished the bicycle project and we presented it in the fair and also at the school assembly. It was a great experience, as I had never presented to such a big crowd, which made me more confident in myself, and we learned that we have to work as a team and not to fight to see who is better, as if we spend time like that, we would make nothing but to fail.

People

There are lots of things to talk about Mexican people and I think they are the most interesting part of this country.

Mexican people are very religious. Nearly all of my schoolmates were baptized to be a Catholic when they were just born of one month. It is said that Mexico holds the second highest number of Catholic. Some of my schoolmates have other religion, but they are as religious as the Catholics, some even go to the church every day. When you talk with your Mexican friend "See you tomorrow," instead of replying " See you then ", they will always say " Si Dios Quiere " which means if God permits. You may feel odd to hear that at first, but when you get used to it and think a little bit about it, you'll understand. To their opinion, God has control over everything and one's destiny is in his hands. Therefore, anything you want to do, it must be done in God's will.

Most of the Mexican people are friendly and polite, they are easy to get along with. They are hospitable. They like to say " my home is your home", which makes you feel very warm. They also very often say " Don't worry " to let you feel at ease when you do something wrong.

Mexican people are physically diverse. Generally speaking, northern people are whiter-skinned and southern people are darker-skinned. And I should say that there is discrimination among them, white-skinned people look themselves superior to darker-skinned people, who are perceived as the lower level.

Mexican people like very much watching television, you'll notice that a typical Mexican home has a family room which is a television room, and apart from it, every bedroom has a television as well, even in a baby's bedroom. My mom always complains about how expensive books are in Mexico, maybe that's why people cannot afford reading books and prefer to watch television.

Mexican people are optimistic. They are not that worried like Asian people do, that's why you feel relaxed being with them. Many of my parents' Chinese friends who used to live in Mexico will miss the life in Mexico when they went back to China.

Mexican people are warm-hearted, willing to help, even when they are busy or don't know how they will still tend to give you a hand. However, this is a big one amongst many Mexicans and can bring some problems, in particular, if you get lost on the street and ask for directions. Rather than telling you they don't know, they'll instead provide a roundabout set of directions, together by a vague wave down the street, in what may or may not be the direction you need to go. So you always need to ask several people to get the right direction. If you take it positively, you'll understand they just don't like to let you down when you need a hand.

Bullying

Campus bullying in Mexico is a sad topic. There are reports that Mexico's campus bullying is one of the worst in the world, but I don't think it is so bad. As I mentioned before, my parents changed many schools for my brother and me during these years, but not because of bullying, they just wanted to get better educational resources for us so long as they could afford. I don't know if public schools are worse since I've never been there. Some say that there is no much difference between public school and private school.

In all the schools I have stayed in, there are really cases of theft, from school uniforms to stationery, pocket money, etc; some students have been nicknamed without consent. However, I've never met students who have been arguing fiercely, or fighting with others; I have never seen anyone abused someone because of his or her rase, family economic conditions, etc. In general, my classmates are very well-educated. Maybe some people are weird, but as long as you can find the right way to get along with them, they are still very friendly.

However, I did experience bullying in my second year of elementary school. At that time I was interested in soccer. To be honest, I'm not athletic talented at all, but since many of my classmates have joined the soccer team, I also want to have a try. Once I was playing as a goalkeeper, I didn't notice the ball coming towards the goal and fail to stop it. My team lost and everybody got mad with me. They accused me of saying that I was a fool and useless. I was deeply hurt and ever since that day, I didn't play soccer anymore. I turned to hate soccer, I refused to watch any soccer game. Well, when I look back on this experience today, I'll think that if this had happened now, I wouldn't let their words affect my life. Today, I don't like watching soccer game just because I don't like it, not because of the fear of been blamed. However, for a 6-year-old kid, the accusation from his peers may really kill him.

Culture

Mexican culture is perhaps one of the most fascinating cultures worldwide. The mixture of strong native legends, artistic expressions, and Spanish culture elements make the Mexican culture unique.

More than eighty percent of the population speaks Spanish. But, Mexican Spanish is unique, quite different than Spanish of Spain. Not only the pronunciation but also phrases and expression style. Even if you know something about Spanish of Spain, you'll still need to take some time to get used to the Mexican Spanish. Whatsmore, you'll often hear people speak in "minority languages," among which Nahuatl is the most important, the next are Maya, Mixteco, and Zapoteco.

Mexican art is also unique and distinct. Mayan traditions are still present in society and it might be best represented in paintings. The most influential artists are Frida Kahlo, who is recognized as one of Mexico's vibrant painters, and her husband Diego Rivera, who painted in 1934 a well-known mural in Rockefeller Center in New York City. Folk art traditions are also well rooted in Mexican culture. Handcrafted ornaments like clay pottery, garments with angular designs and multi-colored baskets and rugs. My dad is fascinated with handmade masks, every time we went on vacations to the "magic towns" and beaches, he will buy a mask. He has a collection of different styles of masks.

Mexican culture is full of legends. Some of them are quite famous, such as the legend of "La Llorona," which means "The Weeping Woman," a woman whose spirit still cries for her lost son; another is the legend of the Sacred woods of Chapultepec, where Aztec emperors had their effigies sculpted in order to achieve immortality. Perhaps one of the key legends present in the Mexican culture is that of Quetzalcoatl. It is said that Quetzalcoatl while searching for the bones he needed to create mankind, reached Mictlan (means "the region of the dead"), where the evil god Mictlantecutli tried to stop him. Aided by his sacred bees and worms, Quetzalcoatl was finally able to get the precious bones and he used them to bring the humankind into the world. The pronunciation of the names are a little bit complicated, but they sound pretty cool, don't you think?

When thinking of music and dance in the Mexican culture, a colorful Mariachi band might come to mind. Mariachi is a folk style of music played by 5 musicians wearing a "charro" suit. They are most memorably heard playing a popular song called " La Cucaracha," which translates to "the Cockroach," on the street, at festivals or in restaurants.

When talking about Mexican culture, you cannot miss the Lady of Guadalupe, who is the patron saint of Mexico. The Guadalupe name and image are national symbols and widely honored. According to a legend, the name Guadalupe was chosen by the Virgin herself. December 12th is the Guadalupe Day, also called the Feast of Lady of Guadalupe. It is considered the most important religious holiday for Mexico. People from all over the country walk a long way from their hometown to the Basilica of Lady of Guadalupe, which is located in Mexico City. The basilica is the world's third most-visited sacred site.

There are much more to talk about Mexican culture, it is a blend of three influences: Native American culture, Spanish culture, and the unique Mexican culture that has developed over time. The Plaza of Three Cultures in Mexico city symbolizes these traditions.

Mexico In My Eyes

Mexico is a country that chronically misunderstood. There are so many falsities and out lies about it. Unfortunately, most people have a wholly negative impression of Mexico.

The most common stereotype statement is "Mexico is Dangerous," it's probably the most enduring untruth about a country that, on the whole, is absolutely fine. I'm not saying that there aren't dangerous parts of Mexico that should probably be avoided, but the same goes for other countries as well. So long as you have an opportunity to come and visit Mexico, not just for sightseeing, but live for a while in order to get to her better, you'll come to understand that it's very different to what the headlines would have you believe.

Mexicans are very proud of their country. This generally relates to the culture and people, not to the nation-state and government. Many Mexicans feel their country has great cultural depth and wealth in comparison to others. There is a saying: "Como Mexico no hay dos," which means there is none other like Mexico. It reflects how people believe Mexico has a particular uniqueness. Mexicans are very proud of the Mesoamerican legacies, such as the Aztecs and Mayans, and are often well educated on the events on history that shaped the identity of their society. For instance, I had a Mexican history class all through my elementary school years.

Mexico may not look like a wealthy country on the outside but on the inside, the people have a heart of gold with high family values and high moral standards. Mexico is a country very rich in history and culture, as well as in natural resources. Mexico is not the best country in the world and it won't be, but she is unique and it is her people that make it so special.

Viva Mexico!

References

1. facts-about-mexico.com
2. bbcgoodfood.com--Top 10 foods to try in Mexico
3. thewholeworldornothing.com---11 common misconceptions about Mexico
4. whatsupsancarlos.com--Mexican Birthday Traditions
5. theculturetrip.com

I want to thank Pixabay for letting me to put free images into this book, which obviously make the text description more vivid and therefore, give the book emotion and feelings.

"Pixabay Stunning Free Images."
Sea ⬜⬜ Bottom Photocomposition ·
Free Image on Pixabay, pixabay.com/.

About the Author

The Author Owen Xu, a 14-year-old teenager, is a Chinese born in Mexico. He uses his unique experience of growing up in Mexico to show people what a real Mexico is in his eyes. He wants to express his genuine love for this beautiful country, to show his respect to the amazing culture and tradition, so that people will get to know better Mexico and her people.

In addition to writing, Owen Xu is passionate about environmental and endangered animal protection. He founded his own organization called ELF Organization, dedicating in creating a better world where wildlife prospers in healthy lands and oceans

CPSIA information can be obtained
at www.ICGtesting.com
Printed in the USA
BVHW021412210519
548769BV00037B/428/P